# WATCHES,
## The History of Time

## An Extensive Look

SAMUEL JOHNSON

# DESCRIPTION

This book tells the reader about the history of different timepieces, why they are given different names such as the chronograph or the Diver's watch and how they revolutionized human practices in their time. The book has classified 10 different types of watches; Swiss watch, Quartz watch, Radio controlled watch, Chronograph watch, Diver's watch, Pilot's watch, Space watch, Military watch, Sports watch and the Race watch.

Each of the watches discussed above have come from some idea about making a certain practice better than before. These watches have served to make life easier for man in his pursuit to achieve success.

The book starts off with an introduction where a brief history of the watch is discussed. The first inventor of the wristwatch (though there is not widespread agreement on who invented it), a wrist watch given as a gift to the Queen of England, and afterwards to the Queen of Naples and how that made the wristwatch become a fashion statement for women. Then the history of the wristwatch takes it turn to a more practical use; War. It was used by soldiers on the battlefield in order to coordinate and time attacks. This led to the wrist watch being manufactured for Mass Production. The Garstin Company was the first to patent a watch design. The watch was used by the British in their colonial struggle. Afterwards, the discussion shifts towards the design changing overtime, simple leather straps and bulky watch faces becoming thinner and sleeker. The wristwatch overtime became desirable for men as well after soldiers were recognized by watches on their wrists. The introduction hints further in the book about how WWl and WWll revolutionized watch-making.

The first chapter is about Swiss watches. A thorough introduction is given about Swiss watches, the history of how the wristwatch became so central to Swiss national identity and how the Swiss were the first in most major watch innovations, such as the first watch-maker's guild, the first perpetual watch, the first waterproof watch and the first quartz watch all came from Switzerland. Further, a discussion on how the Swiss prioritized looks over timekeeping when they made a watch, and the effort they exerted in the fashioning of each timepiece. Moreover, Daniel Jean Richard's innovation in watch-making practices revolutionized the Swiss watch manufacturing process, and the idea of the *Establisseur* came into being.

The second chapter informs the reader about the Quartz watch. The pioneer company in this technology Seiko invented a Quartz watch that was used to time events in the 1964 Tokyo Summer Olympics. A general idea about how a Quartz operates in the watch and regulates the gears within it. Further, Quartz being the reason behind the fall of Swiss global hegemony over wristwatches and the mechanical watch soon becoming a luxury item is outlined as well, which strengthened Japanese and American watch companies.

The third chapter talks about the technology of Radio controlled watches, the watches are relatively a new breakthrough, but have allowed the user the comfort to never having to set their watches again. Junghans is considered the first in inventing a radio controlled watch, and Citizen being the first Japanese brand to experiment with this technology. A brief note on the atomic watch is also within this chapter which can keep time accuracy of one second in 1000 years.

The fourth chapter called Chronograph watches credits Louis Moinet as its inventor. The chronograph history and the role of King Louis IVIII of France in making it sophisticated is discussed. The chronograph became very popular in the world of racing and watch companies started to focus production according to the demands of the race track. Further, how the chronograph operates, its variations; the Flyback and the Rattrapante and how they operate is discussed as well. Lastly a major innovation called the automatic chronograph is also touched upon which was invented by the joint collaboration of

Breitling, Heuer and Hamilton.

The fifth chapter is about the Diver's watch which is designed for underwater diving. Obviously, a brief history about diver's watches is provided where the first diver's watches were worn within the hard hat helmet by the diver. The Rolex Oyster and the Submariners as well as the Omega marine and the submariner are considered pioneer wrist watches that provided water resistance for hundreds of meters. After wards, the ISO 6425 standard is talked about which is an international standard that provides benchmarks to watchmakers that they have to adhere to in order to establish authenticity of their watches. The complete standard is discussed and the benchmarks it provides are also outlined in this chapter. The sixth chapter is about Pilot's watches. The pilot's watch is dated back to the year 1904 when Louis Cartier made an experimental watch for his friend Alberto Santos-Dumant; and early aviator. The role of WWI was essential in innovating the pilot's watch when it was used as a navigation instrument. Charles Lindbergh when he crossed the Atlantic wore a Longines. WWII was when pilot's watches were produced by watchmakers specifically. Hitler's company Luftwaffe made the B-Uhr which had to be returned to the company after the pilot landed from his flight. Radio controlled watches are also born from pilot's watches. Two watches with innovative features made especially for pilots by companies such as Breitling and Citizen are also discussed.

The seventh chapter is about Space watches that need to be robust and highly durable to undergo the demanding experience of outer space travel. Eisenhower ordered astronauts to wear chronographs when NASA evolved in space travel. The Omega Speedmaster, the first watch to go into space saved the lives of the astronauts onboard the Apollo 13.

The eighth chapter is about military watches. They became famous after officers in the army started wearing them. German emperor Wilhelm was the first to introduce military timepieces to the German

Imperial Navy. The hack second hand was invented specifically for troops to synchronize their watches with each other. Further characteristics of the contemporary military watch are discussed.

The ninth chapter talks about Sports watches. These watches come with different sensors and recent electronic sports watches with a number of sensors are also touched upon. The different types of watches catering to a particular sport such as surfing and hiking as well as cycling are discussed.

The tenth chapter talks about Race watches, and the involvement of Rolex and Tag Heuer with Formula One. The Rolex Daytona is named after one of the world's most famous endurance races. Heuer was involved in making timers for the dashboard of the rally and race cars.

The book ends on the note that though in the world of smart watches, the mechanical watch should not be belittled because it has made human progress possible.

# CONTENTS

# INTRODUCTION

Since the dawn of civilization, time has passed either too quickly or slowly so that once could come to terms with. In order to better take this beast, devices were created that indicated the time of day. As science progressed, that time of day become further translated into hours, minutes and seconds. Now though, it is essential for humans to be aware of time because it is time around which our schedules and appointments are set. Thus, it is essential that man be aware of it. And to manage it, the watch came into existence. According to "A history of American Inventions" the first inventor of the watch was a Nuremberg inventor by the name of Peter Heinlein, but that too is contested for ancient history tells us of examples of timepieces being invented even before his time. The wrist watch however was created by Abraham-Louis Breguet for the Queen of Naples somewhere in the 1800s. Even before that, a picture that had surface and immediately became very famous was of a 1926 Gruen Gildt advert where the Earl of Leicester presented a gift to Queen Elizabeth in 1571. It was a highly jeweled arm bracelet with a watch enclosed within it.

Wrist watches initially were just a fashion statement for women. They were placed in the center of bracelets that were usually decorated with gem stones and gold embellishments. Rarely, were they worn by men, because back then the favorite for men was a pocket watch.

It was not until late 19th century when British colonialism began to take hold, it suddenly became important for military men to wear watches, because it was impractical for soldiers to check their pocket watches while they were in the heat of battle.

In 1893 a company in London by the name of Garstin Company successfully patented a design for the wrist watch. In the Boer war these watches became famous in the officer class of the British military. Later, in the 1898 campaign of Sudan by the British military,

Mappin and Webb started production of wrist watches then known as a "soldier watch".

These early models were just simple watches that suited a leather strap; they did not have any protection against water, dirt and required considerable effort in maintenance. It was not until the 20th century that the wrist watch became purpose built. The First World War had revolutionized how we now look at wrist watches. The watch was then built to provide accurate time, be shock resistant, watch cases made out of corrosion resistant materials and protection glass made out of crystal.

The wrist watch has had a legacy that extends centuries back. The novice of today doesn't understand the purpose these watches have served to bring about stability and punctuality in the different professions man has performed over the years. It is thus essential that the different watches that have come about as a result of technology advancements, due to a change in military practices or just to cater to the changing tastes in fashion. A thorough overview should be provided for one to understand these different types of watches, how they work, what their history is, and the technicalities they have served to simplify. There are currently ten different types of watches, namely; Swiss watches, chronograph watches, diver watches, military watches, pilot's watches, space watches, sports watches, quartz watches and motor racing watches. Each watch is discussed further with an emphasis on how they revolutionized practices in their respective fields.

# CHAPTER 1: SWISS WATCHES

When it comes to horology; watch-making, the Swiss are synonymous with perfectly crafted, and luxury timepieces. Today Swiss watches are prized all over the world and are the country's third largest export.

Over the years, most major innovations have emanated from this centre of watch-making excellence. The first watch-maker's guild, the first perpetual watch, the first waterproof watch, the first quartz watch etc have all come from this region.

Origins of Swiss watch-making can be traced from as far back as the 16th century. At the time, John Calvin a religious reformer famous for his ascetic standards of living decided that people should not be allowed to wear jewellery. The jewellery-makers faced financial ruin and considering the fact that the watch was the only item in the jewellery category that was allowed to be worn, decided to turn their attention to the art of watch-making, for which there was a steady increase in demand.

By the end of the 16th century, watch-makers of Geneva had established a reputation for making quality desirable products, because in 1601 the Swiss formed the world's first watch-making guild. Thus, history records Geneva as the birthplace of the entire watch-making industry.

The early watches were manufactured to be as aesthetically pleasing as possible; accuracy of time was not the initial attraction of owning a Swiss timepiece, because during this time bulky watches made in Britain were an obvious choice for timekeepers. The Swiss watches were never accurate, but each one was fashioned to be aesthetically pleasing.

Overtime Geneva became crowded with watch-makers. Some settled in from abroad, but mostly the Swiss continued to work on watches as during the prolonged winter season, there was nothing else to do. Manufacturing took place in small houses and was very compartmentalized. A lot of intricate work was involved. It was common for watch-makers in Switzerland to work on one component of a watch, and then have it passed on to another watch-maker who would start working on another component of the watch. There was no standardization in procedure, which is why manufacturing was a long drawn out process with corrections being done to each watch as it passed from one watch-maker to another. Each stage was thus unique.

## 1.1. Division of Labor:

Geneva had become overcrowded from all these watch-makers, so many of them relocated to the Jura Mountains. One of the pioneers in this location was Daniel Jean Richard. He is regarded as someone who introduced watch-making to Jura. Though, the claim has not yet been verified. However, a claim that is true about him is that he introduced the division of labor concept in watch-making. This concept in essence states that large tasks in the watch-making process are broken down in to smaller sub-tasks, each performed by the same person who has been specifically trained for the job. He continues to do the task repeatedly until he perfects his skills.

As well as the streamlining of the build process, he helped to implement standardized tools and machinery as well as strictly controlled apprenticeships ensuring that knowledge could be passed from generation to generation. This specialization of labor and a set of rules and guidelines was a major factor in the elevation of Swiss watch-making to the zenith it now enjoys.

*1.2. The process:*

Sections of watches were built to exact specifications (often by farmers who provided a source of labor during the winter months) and then collected for final assembly in the main workshop. Even today, the industry falls into two groups:

*1. Manufacturers:* they produce all parts of the watch from start to finish

*2. Establishers:* they assemble watches from parts made from groups of sub-contracted craftsmen.


The decades following saw a boom in the industry and the future was shaped by a number of innovations such as self-winding mechanisms and complications like the calendar and the fly back hand.

*1.3. The Geneva Seal:*

In 1886 the Geneva Seal was given legal status after first being introduced earlier in the century to help deal with an industry plagued with counterfeits. Being one of the first forms of hallmarking, it is still used today and is recognized as a label or origin and guarantee of quality for watches made to superior standards.

*1.4. Contemporary Swiss watch-making:*

Today, the Swiss watch-making landscape is divided between companies that carry on the modern equivalent of establissage, chief among them is the ETA. Then there are watch manufacturers from Germany, America, Denmark and even China that are challenging the conventional wisdom: that only Switzerland is capable of producing fine timepieces.

The recent increase in luxury group acquisitions to demonstrate the consolidation that is rampant in the watch business has made it difficult for independent watch-makers to succeed. In 2011, French company Kering acquired a majority stake in the parent company to the 220 year old prestige Swiss brand Girard-Perreguax. In July, this company purchased the 168 years old watch-maker Ulysse Nardin. In 2013, Corum was sold to Haldian Holdings, marking the first time an haute horlogerie brand fell under Chinese ownership.

# CHAPTER 2: QUARTZ WATCHES

One of the many issues with normal wrist watches was that they had to be wound after a while because eventually they stopped telling the time. This was a serious issue, especially for those people that were often out of station, because if the watch was not wound, it would stop telling the time, and would require another watch to give the user a reference point to set their watch according to it. The watches also displayed dubious accuracy when the temperature would change.

In order to solve all these problems, the quartz crystal was added to them. The quartz crystal sits at the centre of the watch. It's made from a chemical compound called silicon dioxide, which makes it piezoelectric. Thus, the quartz can generate a tiny electric current and vibrate at a precise frequency which enables it to regulate the gears in a watch.

The pioneer company in this technology was Seiko. The Japanese company in 1959 placed an order with its daughter company Epson to start developing a quartz wristwatch. The project was so secret that it was codenamed 59A. By the 1964 Tokyo Summer Olympics, Seiko had a working prototype of a portable quartz watch that was used for time measurements throughout the event.

The first quartz watch launched was the Seiko 35 SQ Astron. This at the time was the most accurate watch of the world. Since, the technology of the quartz crystal in the watch was made by the contributions of Japanese, Americans and the Swiss; who had already made a quartz clock after World War 2, the patent could not be established for the quartz movement to be controlled. Thus, this groundbreaking technology was used by watch-makers worldwide, thereby the 100 years of dominance of the mechanical wrist watch come to a standstill within decades.

Accuracy of the watch would increase with the frequency of the crystal used. Back then, the first generation watches had low frequencies of a few kilohertz. However, the power saving use of the LCD in the second generation watch increased the battery life and allowed the crystal frequency to be increased to 32,768 Hz resulting in an accuracy of 5-10 seconds per month.

## 2.1. Quartz Crisis:

For years, the Swiss had established a global hegemony over wrist watches. Thus, prior to the 1970s, the Swiss watch industry had 50% of the worlds watch market. The Swiss, though had always considered the development of mechanical quartz less watches a part of their national identity and thought that moving into quartz watches was unnecessary.

By 1978 quartz watches overtook mechanical watches in popularity, plunging the Swiss watch industry into crisis while strengthening both Japanese and American watch industries.

As a result, of the economic turmoil that ensued, many once profitable and famous Swiss watch houses disappeared.

By 1983, the crisis reached a critical point. The Swiss watch industry had declined to 600 firms. In this time of turmoil someone had to step up the game. A research firm by the same of the Swiss ASUAG group was formed to save the industry. The result was the Swatch, launched in March 1983. This revived Swiss watch-making traditions and within the span of a few years, the Swatch Group had become one of the largest watch manufacturing companies in the world.

# CHAPTER 3: RADIO CONROLLED WATCHES

In the 1990s, Junghans offered the first radio-controlled wristwatch called the MEGA 1. This watch's quartz oscillator is set to the correct time daily by coded radio time signals broadcasted by government-operated time stations. This allows the user to have long term accuracy and does not have to bother with adjusting time now and then.

Citizen was the first Japanese brand to experiment with this technology. After overcoming many hurdles, in 1993 Citizen debuted the world's first multi-band Radio Controlled Timekeeping watch. The antenna, the heart of signal reception sensitivity would be prone to interference from metal watch cases and parts, so the antenna was placed in the center of the dial. The result was a highly distinctive design that boldly highlighted their new technology to ensure accuracy. Overtime, as technology progressed, the antenna was enclosed within the watch, but out of sight. In 2003 they released the first light-powered radio controlled watch with a metal case called the Citizen Eco Drive.

After Citizen's breakthrough, most radio controlled watches produced come from Japan. The Casio Edifice WAVECEPTOR is one such example that can also be used as a sports watch. The

Seiko Prospex MARINEMASTER has gone a step further and comes with satellite controlled time.

Recently, the atomic wristwatch has been created. Invented in 2013 by Bathys Hawaii, the Cesium 133 is the first watch to keep time with an internal atomic clock. This watch contains a tiny cesium atomic clock on a chip. According to Bathys the watch is considered to keep time to an accuracy of one second in 1000 years. Though, due to the large chip, the watch is bulky and rectangular and must be recharged every 30 hours.

# CHAPTER 4: CHRONOGRAPH WATCHES

The word chronograph is a translation of the Greek word "chronos" which means time and the word "graph" which means writing. The reason why the word writing attaches itself here is because the early chronograph came with a pen that was used to mark the dial so that the time elapsed could be indicated. It is credited with Louis Moinet who completed it in 1816. Initially the chronograph was a tool solely used for astronomical purposes.

King Louis the 18th of France commissioned Nicolas Mathieu Rieussec in 1821 to build the first marketable chronograph. Thus, known throughout France as the "watch-maker of the King", he began developing these watches so that King Louis could time horse races. This changed the very way how horse races would be measured. Reaching the finish line faster did not matter anymore because the time taken for a horse to take off from the starting line and reach the end of the race was now recorded. Later, in the mid 1800s an improved version of Rieussec's Chronograph was invented by Adolphe Nicole who inserted a reset button in the watch which allowed the watch to go back to zero. This enabled the recorders in races to conduct measurements in a row.

During the 20th century, the chronographs became increasingly popular in the world of racing. The manufacturers had now started making another addition; the Tachymeter. The tachymeter was a scale that allowed the user to measure a speed based on the time of travel or compute distance that was based on speed. In 1958 Tag Heuer introduced a rotating bezel that served as a tachymeter for easy adjustment.

## 4.1. Fly back:

The fly back is less commonly known as a Retour-en-vol. It allows one to track time in quick succession multiple times without having to reset it manually with another pusher. Unlike a normal chronograph which has to be started, stopped, reset and restarted, the fly back reduces all this to just one action. Once the timer starts, push the button once again and the hand will jump back and start running again. In these watches, the second pusher serves to stop the stopwatch. People credit the invention of the flyback to Breitling but the patent for the flyback chronograph is owned by Longines.

## 4.2. Rattrapante:

The Rattrapante or a double chronograph allows one to make two measurements separatehly but simultaneously, because they have two chronograph seconds hands. The term *"rattraper"* means "to catch up". When the timers are started, both the chronograph hands; the seconds hand and the small hand within the sub-dial start working together. Then if one of the corresponding pusher is squeezed, one of the hands stops moving. Squeezing the pusher again will make the stopped hand jumps back to the starting point. The rattrapante is also known as a split-second because it is useful for measurement of more than a single object, saving time of one measurement while still tracking the other.

## 4.3. The Automatic Chronograph:

In the 1960s, Breitling, Heuer and Hamilton decided to

partner up with movement expert Dubois Depraz, and the first ever self-winding chronograph was invented. It was unveiled in New York and Geneva on March 3, 1969. Known as the Chrono-matic, the Calibre 11 movement would wind itself via an off-center micro rotor. During this time another brand called the Zenith produced a chrono-matic called the "El Primero" which came with a central mounted full rotor and was capable of measuring time to one-tenth of a second. As these two developments came into the market, the Japanese watch-maker Seiko released their own automatic chronograph known as the 6139 Auto-chrono. The importance of the chronograph increased with popular sports throughout the world. It was used in Formula One racing, bike racing, rowing, swimming and other Olympic sports. The watch also became a strategic asset for the navy as they used it for ship and submarine navigation. There were a number of chronographs that were created overtime to make up for the increase in oscillating demands. Two of the most famous were the fly back and the rattrapante.

# CHAPTER 5: DIVER'S WATCHES

The standard diver's watch is designed for underwater diving and features a water resistance greater than 1.0 MPa, the equivalent of 100 m or 330 feet. A typical divers watch has around 200 to 300 m of water resistance. Every diver's watch has to confirm to the ISO 6425 standard. Watches with this confirmation are marked with the word DIVER'S to be distinguished under the same ISO from watches that are not suitable for actual scuba diving.

The water resistant diver's watch started off from the 17th century. These watches initially were described as "Explorer's watches" because they were custom made for particular customers. Back then, scuba divers with hard hat helmets used to dive underwater with pocket watches placed inside their helmets. During the 20th century, these watches started to be produced for commercial distribution.

In 1926 Rolex patented the "Oyster" watch case, which featured an airtight seal. The English swimmer Mercedes Gleitze attempted to cross the English Channel with the watch hanging around her neck. Even though the swim took 10 hours, the watch kept functioning with accurate time throughout.

Omega was the first watch company to produce the diving

watch, made especially for commercial distribution. The Omega "marine" was introduced in 1932 and came with a patented double sliding and removable case. After repeated trials by the Swiss Laboratory for Horology in 1937, the watch was certified to be able to withstand pressure of 1.37 MPa, equivalent to the depth of 135 m or 443 ft.

in 1953 Lip-Blancpain introduced a waterproof watch in France. Various models of the same watch were issued to the combat diver teams of different countries. The watch popularly known as Fifty Fathoms made a movie appearance in the underwater film "Le mondu du silence" and in the US Lloyd Bridges appeared in a photo on the cover of the February 1962 edition of Skin Diver Magazine handsomely suiting the watch. The Rolex Submariner was launched in 1954, and in 1961 they began to include a skin diver handbook with the Submariner. The watch was then available with water resistance of 200m and 100m respectfully. It was also the watch worn in the first ten James Bond movies which gave the Submariner an iconic status. Whereas, after a few years Seiko put the 62MAS on the market. It was the first Japanese professional diver's watch.

During the 1960s, underwater diving had become a thing. Organizationally sanctioned underwater diving was introduced and more robust watches were required. Rolex during this time released an "ultra water resistant" watch known as the Rolex Sea-Dweller 2000 which was able to withstand pressure at abnormal depths of 610m. In competition Omega released the Seamaster Professional which also withstood pressure at depths of 600m.

In 1996 the International Organization for Standardization introduced the standards and features for diving watches regulated by the ISO 6425 Diver's watch International standard. Diving watches were now used by divers to measure the time and depth of a dive so that a safe ascent could be calculated which meant that the diver could avoid decompression sickness.

## 5.1. What is ISO 6425?:

This is a standard regulated by the International Organization for Standardization. The standard provides benchmarks that have to be observed by diving watch-makers. It establishes a minimum benchmark for water resistance of at least a 100m depth, and also provides requirements for mechanical diver's watches that have to be scrutinized before the watch can get the DIVER'S mark. This standard was established because divers undergo unusual circumstances underwater.

The standards are given below:

* The watch should come with a unidirectional bezel with a marking of every 5 minutes elapsed and a marker to establish specific minute marking.

* These minute markings should be clearly distinguishable

* Visibility should be at a minimum 25cm in total darkness.

* There should be an indication that tells the user that the watch is running in total darkness. Luminous material on the second hand satisfies this precondition.

 * The watch should be magnetic resistant. The watch must keep its accuracy despite in a magnetic field.

* The watch should be shock resistant.

* The watch should be chemical resistant. This is tested by immersing the watch in seawater for 24 hours.

* The watch should have a very strong band or strap. This is tested by applying force to each spring bar in opposite directions ensuring that the watch does not receive any

damage.

\* There should be and End of Life (EOL) indicator on battery powered watches

Adhering to the standards is purely voluntary but, watch-makers go through the costs so that the authenticity of their watches is not compromised. Thus, the standards then translate into the characteristics that are fairly common to every diver's watch, every watch comes with a specific set of functions that are useful for when the user is under water or is about to be. Some of the characteristics are:

*5.2. Watch case:*

The watch cases are made of grade 316L or 904L stainless steel and other steel alloys such as titanium, synthetic resins or plastics. The case is also developed with magnetic resistance, and shock protection.

*5.3. Elapsed time controller:*

The diver's watch comes with a rotating bezel that allows the user to read elapsed time. This is mostly used to compute dive length. When the diver is about to enter the water, he aligns the zero on the bezel with the minute or second hand. This way the diver does not have to remember the exact water entry moment and can avoid the calculation involved with a normal dial watch. The bezel is also uni-directional unlike race watches because it provides a fail-safe feature for if the bezel were to rotate the other way from the water pressure the elapsed time will be a false reading. In order to counter these errors most new watches now come with lockable bezels.

*5.4. Glass face:*

When underwater, the pressure of the water on the watch is tremendous. The watch must be built with a glass face that can withstand that pressure and compromise water entry. For this, the diver's watch comes with thick watch crystals. The shape of the glass face can be domed as well to enhance pressure resistance. The materials used can be synthetic sapphire, acrylic glass or hardened glass. Hardened glass resists scratches, acrylic glass resists breakage and sapphire is very scratch resistant. Anti-reflective coatings are applied on sapphire to increase visibility.

## 5.6. Helium release valve:

Watches built for diving at great depths feature this valve; it is also called a mixed breathing gas release valve or escape valve. It prevents the glass face from popping out of the watch by internal pressure built up by helium seeped into the watch case, which increases at greater depths. Some even develop watches with gaskets in them to avoid helium entry.

## 5.7. Watchstrap:

Diver's watches come with watch straps or bracelets that are anti corrosive. Thus, many watches come with a rubber strap or fabric watchstrap. Metal bracelets come with extensions that can be deployed if the user wears the watch on top of a bathing suit. The springs and hinges within the bracelet can also have vented sections that facilitate flexibility when the watch tightens from the pressure underwater.

## 5.8. Visibility:

One of the most important features of the diver's watch is the luminescent pigments that are added into the watch case. The hands and the hour markings are intentionally made luminescent in order to maximize visibility when deep sea diving where visibility is at a minimum.

# CHAPTER 6: PILOT'S WATCHES

The first Pilot's watch dates back to the year 1904 when Alberto Santos-Dumont an early aviator asked his friend Louis Cartier to design a watch that could be used during flight. According to legends, after Santos made his first flight, he was given a German Archdeacon Aviation Prize for the stunt. In the course of celebration, he approached Cartier and told him about the difficulty of using a pocket watch during mid-flight. Cartier then developed and aeronautical watch that served several functions. It could calculate air speed, lift capacity and was useful for time keeping.

The importance of the Pilot's watch was recognized when Louis Bleriot made his first flight across the English Channel. The media talked about it while discussing the fact that Bleriot had a Zenith watch on his wrist.

The first use of the Pilot's watch in war came during World War 1 when they were used as navigation instruments. The purpose of the watch was to make a coordinated attack at a precise moment possible. These were pocket watches called Mark 4 A and Mark 5, the A stood for aviation. The peculiar feature of these watches was a long crown housing. The purpose of that was to make them fit in an instrument panel, thus they became nicknamed as the "cockpit watch".

During the Atlantic flight conducted by Charles Lindbergh, the watch he wore as a navigation tool was a Longines. During the flight, the only way to measure distance covered was to check time and to compensate for the lack of accuracy in watches, a fact common among watches back then. The Longines came with a rotating inner dial that could be set to get rid of accuracy errors. He aligned the dials using beeps coming from the radio, using the beeps as a reference. That was how the rotating bezel came into existence. The Longines watch also allowed the pilot to determine the hour angle with a decent precision.

When World War 2 started, Adolf Hitler established the company Luftwaffe, during that time the ministry of Air Transport in Germany was looking for a standard issue watch that would facilitate bomber crews. The design that was created seemed similar to the Longines issues with the hour angle indication, but the B-Uhr that came out from the labor was starkly different. It is an iconic watch even for today. The B-Uhr or Beobachtungs-uhren (Observation watches) were given to pilots but owned by Luftwaffe. The watch had to be returned after a flight. These watches were also synchronized manually by radio signals, and that laid the foundation for modern day Radio Controlled watches (RC watches).

During the cold war dial faces increased in size. This was partly because pilots had a hard time checking the watch if the dial was too small. This was the time when tritum-lit hands also came into existence. Tritum, being a radioactive isotope is luminous in darkness. They can provide 20 years of luminosity.

One of the most famous watches that came in this time was the Rolex GMT Master. It came with a GMT hand that goes around the dial once every 24 hours. It was set for the London time zone. The bezel included 24 hours on the scale, and if 24 was aligned with 12 on the main dial, then it was possible to see

Greenwich Time. The pilot could rotate the bezel as a point of reference to check different time zones.

Rolex GMT remained a standard issue watch for Pan America pilots for a very long time.

## 6.1. Contemporary watches:

Contemporary watches feature a number of functionalities that are suited specifically for aviation. There are two watches that are currently very popular among pilots throughout the world, specifically for their practicality; the Breitling Emergency and the Citizen Promaster Skyhawk AT JY0080-62E.

The Breitling has a very unique feature that could be considered lifesaving for a pilot if the plane loses control and nosedives. The watch consists of two mechanisms; the first one being a digital chronograph and second time zone display along with an analog dial. The second and the most important feature is that the watch contains a distress beacon with an antenna, which can be used by a downed pilot to call for help. According to Breitling, the watch transmits a first digital signal on the 406 MHz frequency intended for satellites and lasting .44 seconds every 55 seconds, as well as a second analog signal on the 121.5 MHz homing and rescue frequency, lasting .75 seconds every 2.25 seconds. Breitling claims that if the watch is used in a real emergency, it will be replaced for free. That is why it is fairly common to see the watch on the wrists of Western pilots. It is also worn by John Travolta who likes to fly planes when he is not starring in movies.

The second watch; the Citizen Promaster Skyhawk is famous among the Polish Air Force F-16 pilots. It is also capable of numerous aviation related features.

The watch is radio controlled, so there never is a need for setting the time manually, and it has the capability to indicate time for all time zones. The watch includes a chronograph, a timer, two alarms, GMT time and a perpetual calendar. The watch has Eco-Drive solar charging which means that there is never a battery replacement.

The most functional feature of the watch is the "slide-rule" bezel. This allows the user to perform a number of calculations, which includes fuel consumption, unit conversion, square root etc. It is a great aid in navigations.

# CHAPTER 7: SPACE WATCHES

Space watches need to be highly robust and durable watches since space flight is widely agreed as a demanding experience for a watch. It undergoes a variety of stresses. The gravitational pull as the rocket lifts off is 6 times greater than the earth. Thus, the watch should have the ability to withstand a severe change in pressure.

The watches should also be able to withstand extreme temperature fluctuations in outer space that can go to as low as -160 to 120 degrees C. That is why the watches are tested many times before they can pass on to the astronaut's wrist.

President Eisenhower, a renowned watch collector and horologist, had ordered all pilots and astronauts to wear a chronograph as space exploration by NASA evolved.

On April 15, 1970, just 56 minutes after launching and 200,000 miles from Earth, an explosion occurred on the Apollo 13. The shuttle collapsed and NASA believed that this accident would be the certain death of Apollo 13's astronauts. However, the astronauts returned safely to earth on April 17, 1970. The reason was the Omega Speedmaster that they were ordered to wear by President Eisenhower. The astronauts were able to use the chronograph function to time a critical engine burn despite all the onboard computers being fried. As they were able to calculate their reentry to earth, they aligned the capsule which resulted in a safe splashdown. This is partly the reason nowadays that the vast majority of commercial and military pilots wear chronographs, for fear that if their systems fail, they have a simple mechanical watch to save them.

Ever since, the watch has won numerous accolades. The Speedmaster is still in space, because it is adopted by the Russian Federal Space Agency as the standard issue watch for Soyuz crews, and also for cosmonauts at the International Space Station (ISS). Another variation of the watch known as the Speedmaster X33 is also very popular among astronauts as it was seen on the wrist of American astronaut Scott Kelly as he returned to Earth after spending 342 days in space. The watch is designed specifically for space and features a very loud alarm, a light that can almost be used as a flashlight if it's really dark and a GMT time.

Another important aspect of an aerospace watch is something that has evolved from the history of aviation watches. It is the ability to measure air pressure and altitude. Recently, the American Navy has assigned Garmin Fenix 3 watches to their Fighter Squadron pilots so that physical episodes in the cockpit can be prevented.

There are a number of other watches that have been used in outer space time and again, each with its own specifications.

The Pobeda Shturmanskie was worn by Yuri Gagarin when he went into space, because of its high quality and accuracy. Then later, the Strela chronograph Vostok was the second favorite of Russian astronauts.

Another favorite is the Swiss brand Breitling. Scott Carpenter wore his Breitling Navitimer in the Aurora 7 Mission in May 1962. It had a 24 hour display which was useful since the concept of the rising and setting sun is not relevant to astronauts. Later on in the Franco-Russian missions of 1996 and 2001 the Breitling Aerospace was worn by astronauts and it came with an extra long velcro strap that could be adjusted according to the space suit size. It also came with an engraved back and special logo.

Another Swiss watch famous for being worn by American astronaut John Glenn was the Tag Heuer stop watch. It had been modified with elastic bands to cater to the space suit.

Another famous watch is the Rolex GMT Master. It was worn on the Apollo 15 mission by Ron Evans. The watch is further acclaimed for being worn by Chuck Yeager when he was the first person to pilot a fixed wing plane to the speed of sound, when no one knew whether a plane, a human or this watch could endure such forces.

# CHAPTER 8: MILITARY WATCHES

Initially the wrist watch in general was used by the military. It became famous after officers from the army started wearing them. The first watch produced for the military began to appear in the1800s. German emperor Wilhelm the first was one of the few to introduce military timepieces when he ordered thousands of them to be produced specifically for the German Imperial Navy. By the 20th century, military commanders throughout the world had figured out the utility of timekeeping in battle. That was when military watches were issued directly with uniforms to the troops.

Early wrist watches were a modification of the pocket watch, they were fashioned by welding hinges to the side of the pocket watch and a leather strap was attached to either side which could be adjusted according to wrist size. This feature was added so that the soldier could coordinate attacks with precision and cooperation like never before. The British army used it in battles throughout their colonial struggle.

The concept of wearing a watch became popular when soldiers would come home wearing a wristwatch, the soldier was identified by his wrist watch, and soon this became a fashion symbol that was gradually adopted by the general public. To meet this growing trend, watch-makers began to innovate wrist watches, they became thinner and more sleek with different features added to them, such as the date/time feature.

Just as watch-makers changed their wrist watch concepts to accommodate the general public, the ever changing dynamics of the battle field also required them to implant innovations in the military watch. The "hack" second hand started to be incorporated in military watches. Troops in the field required a way to synchronize their watches between artillery gunners and the infantry advancing behind the barrage, so a movement was designed that gave the user the option to stop the second hand by pulling out the crown. Another innovation was the compass being incorporated into the watch, so that platoons could navigate in unfamiliar areas and coordinate with nearby helicopters to settle a rendezvous point.

## 8.1. Characteristics of the contemporary military watch:

The contemporary military watch has been built to suit a myriad of issues that troops face when they go into the field. The recent military watch comes equipped with sensors like barometer, altimeter and the compass. Military watches are built with high grade titanium in order to withstand rough use.

Watches such as the Suunto Ambit 3 comes with a heart monitor infused within the watch so that troops can measure their heart rate during early morning training. The Suunto Ambit 2 as well as the 3 comes with GPS that can provide the troops location, this is especially important in areas where lines of communication are severed. Some of the watches such as the 5.11 field watch especially made for the military comes with a high density polycarbonate case, integrated compass, backlight that can be toggled, calculators, wrist band extensions for if one is wearing gloves or a jacket, water resistance, audible alerts and even a 45 month battery EOL for those troops that live for extended periods in remote locations.

# CHAPTER 9: SPORTS WATCHES

There was another watch on Commander Scott Kelly's wrist as well when he came out of the capsule after landing on earth. Though it would seem pale in comparison to the Omega that stood by its side, but it has a utility that was essential to Scott Kelly. It was an actigraph that monitors sleep and rest cycles. These types of watches have found quite a market in recent years for various reasons. They are worn by athletes, gym goers and sportsmen. While suiting an actimetry sensor, they also contain other sensors that measure distance travelled, heartbeat, and calories burned. These watches come with built in chips, digital screens, Bluetooth sensors, can be charged with a USB and then continue to function for a week. But before there were cell phones that connect to watches, and the technology available, there were watches that catered to sportsmen. Where the watches lacked in technology, they compensated for being engineering marvels.

The chronograph, the tachymeter, the split-function, night mode and water resistance are all such features that are useful to sports enthusiasts. These were functions that were brought about in classic watches by Rolex, Omega, Zenith, Breitling, and Piguet.

The first example of a sports watch was the Rolex Submariner which came with night mode, tachymeter, and the highest water resistance depth of watches of the time. But Rolex has had a long history of being worn by golf's greatest players. Phil Mickelson winner of five major championships including three Masters Titles and the 2013 PGA Tournament wears a Rolex Oyster Perpetual Day-Date. Arnold Palmer, Tiger Woods and Jack Nicklaus all own a Rolex.

But the father of modern sports watches that operated electronically was the Casio G-SHOCK. The watch was invented by a frustrated Casio engineer who did not approve of the fragility of mechanical watches. So he decided to make a watch that would be capable of resisting real abuse. It took 3 years and more than a hundred prototypes for the G-Shock DW5000 to be born in 1983. The watch was tested by being dropped from a fourth floor men's bathroom window. Further, the watch was made of tough rubber, had a 100 m water resistance, impervious to shock, featured a night-mode and had a ten year battery life.

## 9.1. Contemporary electronic sports watches:

The Sunnto Ambit that has been mentioned previously is the ideal watch for the sports enthusiasts. The watch includes an online planning and analysis tool as well which allows the user to keep a sports diary.

Nowadays, electronic watches come equipped with functions that cater to a particular watch in order to establish permanence. An example of this is the Nixon Supertide, which has sunrise and sunset data for over 230 beaches worldwide; it even updates the user of the motion of the waves. Then, there is the Columbia Switchback that is built for hikers and athletes. It can read temperature, has an advanced GPS, as well as a 50-lap memory and a chronograph. The G-Shock Lap Memory has similar features as well, and a sensor that illuminates the watch when the user faces it. The Timex Ironman Run Trainer is built for cyclists that can switch modes from cycling to running at the push of a button. It can also measure distance traveled both on bike and foot, as well as a heartbeat sensor. Whereas the most unique watch at the moment is the Tissot Racing Touch that is both a combination of mechanical and electronic wrist watches. It comes with a touch-screen surface, which enables the user to check split times and change routes at a simple touch. It has dual time zone capabilities, a compass for hiking, a tide calculator, night mode and a special logbook feature that saves up to 99 lap times. The watch though is relatively expensive as compared to its competitors, but it is no doubt a rebirth of the classic wristwatch that has been tweaked enough to keep up with modern times.

# CHAPTER 10: RACE WATCHES

One of the few reasons why wrist watches and motor racing have become inseparable are because motor racing highly depends on accurate timekeeping. It is essential for recording lap times, race times and other data. In fact, the 1894 Paris-Rouen Le Petit Journal "Competition for Horseless Carriages" widely regarded as the world's first motor race, finished with several different sets of race times because of poor timekeeping.

It was not until the early 1930s that wristwatches became widely used in racing. Rolex was one of the first to capitalize on this market after Sir Malcolm Campbell set a new land speed record attempt at Bonneville, Utah in 1935 while wearing a Rolex Oyster.

Though, Rolex was the first watch used in motor sports racing, Tag Heuer is that name that comes to mind when Formula One and racing is discussed. That is because it was closely associated with racing throughout the second half of the 20th century. Heuer was involved in making timers for the dashboard of the rally and race car. It was not uncommon to see the Master Time and the Monte Carlo imbedded in dashboards. Especially through the 1950s, Ferrari, Lotus, Maserati and other leading Formula One teams depended on manually-wounded Heuer chronographs to record their drivers.

Heuer continued making its big three chronographs-the Autavia, Carrera and Monaco to make them appeal to drivers. The watches turned automatic from manual in 1969 and it earned Heuer's Caliber 11 the title of the "first automatic chronograph". Steve McQueen wore a Monaco 1133 in Le Mans during the 1970s. During this decade, Heuer also developed an Automatic Car Identification Timing (ACIT) system, which was capable of simultaneously recording the times of multiple cars using micro transmitter technology. ACIT is still used in the world of racing.

It wasn't just the Heuer though. The iconic Omega Speedmaster was also originally designed as a sports and racing chronograph. The Rolex Daytona is named after one of the world's most famous endurance races.

Even today, Swiss watch-makers continue to provide timekeeping for many of the world's most acclaimed racers. TAG Heuer, Longines, Hublot and most recently, Rolex have taken the title of Official Time Keepers for Formula One racing.

# CONCLUSION

The different types of watches above are used to tell time, measure distances and understand time zones. They have passed through a lot of hurdles to compete with modern times and have gone from being simple time tellers to carrying features like chronographs, tachymeters, different time zones, night mode, water resistance and the ability to withstand the pursuits of the ever busy human wrist.

Truth be told, every watch that is now used for different purposes came from man's struggle to pursue the impossible. These watches took time and unquestionable discipline, and a serious amount of concentration. They became part of a tradition that has now spanned centuries, the Swiss took it far and made it a way of life. Nowadays, we pick up our smart watches such as the apple watch or the Samsung gear and use it to take pictures and write messages, but these watches are born from an immense struggle that has stretched through millennia by watchmakers to provide the perfect timepiece.

It would thus be demeaning to look at these masterpieces with skepticism because they have brought about a revolution in the human pursuit to achieve greatness. Whether it was Mercedes Gleitze's attempt to cross the English Channel with a Rolex around her neck, the British attempts to advance in Burma and Sudan, Scott Kelly's attempt to spend almost an year in space, Steve McQueen's race against time in Le Mans, Chuck Yeager's endeavor to reach the speed of sound, or Sir Malcolm Campbell's successful feat when he achieved the worlds quickest land speed record. All these high points have been achieved with the help of a normal mechanical watch guiding them.

The classic watch still beats the test of time for when there is no technology in the dusty desert or the thick wilderness, the wristwatch will be the trusted companion.

Printed in Great
Britain
by Amazon